MW00772612

Seven Principles of

SINGLE-SESSION THERAPY

Seven Principles of
SINGLE-SESSION THERAPY

Windy Dryden, PhD

Rationality Publications

Rationality Publications
136 Montagu Mansions, London W1U 6LQ

www.rationalitypublications.com
info@rationalitypublications.com

First edition published by Rationality Publications
Copyright (c) 2021 Windy Dryden

The right of Windy Dryden to be identified as the author of
this work has been asserted in accordance with sections 77
and 78 of the Copyright Designs and Patents Act 1988.

A catalogue record of this book is
available from the British Library.

First edition 2021

ISBN: 978-1-910301-92-0

Contents

Introduction

This is the third book in the 'Seven Principles' series, where I discuss seven key principles that explain the essence of a particular therapeutic topic. This book outlines the seven key principles of Single-Session Therapy (SST) as I see them.

In *Principle 1*, I discuss the nature of SST and the importance of the therapist agreeing with the client that the latter wants to proceed on the basis that the therapist will help them in one session, but that more help is available if the client wants it.

Following this, I discuss the view that SST needs to be understood within the context in which it is practised. Thus, in *Principle 2*, I consider SST by walk-in and by appointment and various ways in which SST can be offered to clients within agencies.

In *Principle 3,* I outline what is known as the single-session mindset (or single-session thinking) and contrast this with a more conventional clinical mindset. I argue that practitioners can hold multiple mindsets and need to use the single-session mindset when practising SST rather than conventional clinical thinking.

In *Principle 4*, I discuss a process view of SST and make the point that the session is best viewed as complete in itself and has a beginning, a middle and an end. It is definitively not several sessions condensed into one.

In *Principle 5,* I present ideas about what constitutes a good working alliance in SST. In doing so, I describe the four components of the alliance: bonds, views, goals and tasks – and show how the SST practitioner strives to develop and sustain a good working relationship with the client in each of these four components during the session.

Effective work in SST is based on implementing a set of consensually agreed ways of practice, together with a set of more individual practice contributions. In *Principle 6,* I focus on the consensual set of practice methods, while in *Principle 7,* I discuss what individual therapists can bring to the SST process. In doing so, and for illustrative purposes, I discuss what I bring to SST as an individual practitioner.

At the end of the book, I present a brief further reading list for those who want to study SST in greater depth. I hope you find this book of value.

Windy Dryden
March 2021

PRINCIPLE 1

Agreeing on the Nature of Single-Session Therapy (SST)

In this first principle, I will begin by considering the nature of single-session therapy and then discuss the importance and therapeutic power of the therapist and client agreeing to go forward based on a mutual understanding of what the therapist can do and cannot do in SST.

The Ronseal Definition: One-Session SST

At first glance, it may seem obvious what the nature of single-session therapy (SST) is. It is one session of therapy, no more, no less. This is what I call the Ronseal definition of SST.[1] Indeed, there are some circumstances when SST does last for one session without any other further contact between therapist and client.

---

[1] Ronseal is a company that makes wood-staining products. They are perhaps best known for their catchy advertising phrase: 'Ronseal, it does exactly what it says on the tin.'

Therapy Demonstrations

When I give a demonstration of therapy with a volunteer at a professional workshop or webinar in front of an actual or online audience, then this is the only time that I will be seeing the person for therapy. The volunteer knows this also. This is an example of SST where there is an agreement between the volunteer and myself that we will only have one therapy session. Some people refer to this as a 'one-off' session. When I call for a volunteer, I say something like, 'Please volunteer if you have a genuine, current problem for which you would like to seek help. Please choose an issue that you are prepared to discuss in front of an audience of your peers.' I generally record the session with the volunteer's agreement and offer them, by request, the recording of the session and later a transcript of the session.[2]

Regular Therapy Practice

There may be times in regular therapy practice where a person may contact the therapist with the expressed intention of having only one session with the therapist. This may be for one of several reasons.

---

[2] While this is my regular practice, other therapists who do therapy demonstrations do not do this.

'I only need one session': The client may think that the issue they are bringing to therapy can be dealt with in one session and, therefore, they are only prepared to commit to one session. It is important that the client makes this clear at the outset, for not all therapists are willing or prepared to practise SST under these circumstances, so the therapist needs to give their informed consent to proceed.[3]

Client ambivalence about therapy – a 'trial' session: A person may be ambivalent about seeking help from a therapist and only be prepared to have one session to see what it is like. Again, it is vital that the person is transparent about what they are looking for so that the therapist can give their informed consent and respond accordingly. My practice under these circumstances is to agree to the 'trial' session but to assume that this *may* be the only time that I will be seeing the client and to 'run' the session as a one-off session of SST.

A single-session of concurrent therapy: The third reason for a person only committing to one session of therapy is when this person is consulting another therapist but is seeking assistance on an issue with

---

[3] While the concept of informed consent is more frequently discussed as something given by the client, it also applies to the therapist as shown here.

which that therapist has not been able to help them. With the first therapist's agreement, the person seeks help from a second therapist in the form of a single session. It is important that the second, single-session therapist knows the reason for the consultation and agrees. At the end of the single session, the client returns to the first therapist to continue the work that they have been doing with that person.

More Help Is Available If Needed

While single-session therapy can mean one session and one session only, with no pre-session preparation contact and no follow-up contact, it more often means something different. A typical definition of single-session therapy is as follows: 'Single-session therapy is a purposeful endeavour where both parties set out with the intention of helping the client in one session knowing that more help is available if needed.'

What makes this single-session therapy is the *agreed intentionality* of the work. In other words, the therapist and client agree that they will both strive to get the job done in one session. However, this intentionality is placed in a broader context. First, it encompasses what has been referred to as 'a pre-session preparation contact' where the client and therapist have a brief opportunity to prepare for the session to help the client get the most from the session.[4] Second, it incorporates a follow-up contact whereby the therapist has an opportunity to discover how the client has been getting on and if they need further help. This last point reflects the idea that is central to single-session therapy, namely that more help is available if required.

What Help is Available and How to Access It?

One of the possible problems with the 'more help is available' part of the definition of SST is that it is said glibly without due concern about what specific help is available to the client in the agency at which the client has sought help, for example. Thus, the therapist needs to be transparent about what help is available and what is not available both at the beginning of the SST process and towards the end of the session when it is becoming clear that the client is likely to need or request more help. Besides, when an agency offers the service that the client has asked for at the end of the session, it is again important that the therapist is transparent about the likely period that the client will have to wait to access this service.

---

[4] This preparation work can be done interactively, for example by telephone or it can be done by the client completing a questionnaire which is shared with the therapist before the session.

How Do Clients Find Out about SST and What Is Disseminated?

After an agency or a therapist in independent practice has decided to add SST to the range of services they offer, they need to grapple with disseminating SST so that potential clients can understand what SST is and how they can access it if they are interested. There are two ways agencies and independent practitioners can disseminate information about SST: websites and leaflets.

Websites

Most agencies and independent practitioners have websites, which provide a vital opportunity for disseminating SST as a service.[5]

Leaflets

While somewhat 'old school', leaflets still have a place in today's dissemination of single-session therapy. They can be left in GP surgeries and sent as an email attachment to interested parties. Appendix 1 presents the leaflet that I have designed and which

---

[5] One of the best websites that I have found concerning the dissemination of SST is that hosted by Relationships Australia Victoria. See https://www.relationshipsvictoria.com.au/services/counselling/SSC (accessed 12 February 2021).

I send out to people seeking more information about SST.

Whiteboard Animation

A modern way of disseminating information about SST is by a whiteboard animation. This is a video that shows the viewer images being drawn on the screen. The illustrations are accompanied by a narration that talks the audience through the story being told within the drawing. I have developed a whiteboard animation explaining SST which is on YouTube (https://www.youtube.com/watch?v=wIcuOV OABRw).[6] Appendix 2 presents the narration of this whiteboard animation video.

Therapist Transparency at the Outset

There may be times when a person presents themself for SST without being fully informed of the nature of SST. One of the ways in which I begin SST, especially when I have not had prior contact with the person, is to ask them, 'What is your understanding of the purpose of our conversation today?' If the person's response is consistent with the aims and nature of SST, then we can proceed. If not, I explain what SST is and what I can do and what I can't do as a therapist within an SST context. After which, the

---

[6] Accessed on 12 February 2021.

person can decide whether or not they want to have the session.

*

In this principle, I have discussed the nature of single-session therapy and made the point that the therapist and client need to agree on its nature to proceed. Before I discuss single-session thinking and the practice that flows from this thinking, it is important to consider SST in the context in which it is practised. This is the focus of *Principle 2*.

PRINCIPLE 2

Viewing SST in Context

Single-Session Therapy is not an approach to therapy in the same way that CBT or person-centred therapy is, for example. Instead, SST is a way of thinking about therapy and a service delivery mode (Young, 2018). In this principle, I will discuss the service delivery context of SST. In the following principle, I will discuss single-session thinking or what some refer to as the single-session mindset.

Single-Session Therapy by Walk-In

In the UK, we have a tradition of drop-in centres within the context of mental health. Here, a person 'drops-in' to a mental health centre, is greeted, usually by a volunteer, offered a cup of tea or coffee and invited to take a look around and read appropriate material, if interested. After a while, the person is asked if they would like a brief chat with someone, which is to determine the reason for the person's visit and signpost relevant forms of help if the discussion goes in that direction. The drop-in is there to welcome the visitor, offer a de-stigmatising environment for people with mental health issues, provide information and assist with appropriate signposting of most relevant services. While such drop-in centres play an important role in mental health, as detailed above, they are not walk-in centres as these are defined within the SST community.

A single-session based walk-in service provides the person who 'walks-in' to the service with a single therapy session. This is made clear on the agency's website and within the community. The following quote, which is my favourite short piece of writing in the entire SST literature, makes the nature of an SST walk-in centre abundantly clear. Walk-in therapy

> enables clients to meet with a mental health professional at their moment of choosing. There is no red tape, no triage, no intake process, no wait list, and no wait. There is no formal assessment, no formal diagnostic process, just one hour of therapy focused on clients' stated wants....Also, with walk-in therapy there are no missed appointments or cancellations, thereby increasing efficiency.
>
> (Slive, McElheran and Lawson, 2008: 6)

Such walk-in centres are quite common in Canada, Australia and the USA. However, they are not common in the United Kingdom. My thoughts about this are that when people think of such walk-in services (as opposed to drop-in centres), they do so from the perspective of conventional thinking about providing mental health services instead of the perspective of single-session thinking to be described in *Principle 3*.

Given that these walk-in centres are not prevalent in the UK, I will not describe them in further detail but refer the interested reader to the work of Arnie Slive and Monte Bobele, two pioneers of the field of walk-in therapy (see Slive and Bobele, 2011).

Single-Session Therapy by Appointment

Single-session therapy by walk-in is the most efficient example of help provided at the point of need (rather than at the point of availability). Single-session therapy by appointment attempts to preserve this 'help provided at the point of need' approach. Still, there is a short wait for the appointment compared to the immediacy of the help offered in walk-in centres.

If a therapy agency provides single-session therapy as a mode of service delivery, it is likely that it will sit alongside other forms of help provided by that agency. The question then becomes how does a person end up accessing SST in a multi-service delivery agency? The following are different ways of answering this question.

The Person Chooses SST

One way of approaching the question of how a person accesses SST is for them to choose SST from a range of services that an agency offers. Here, the agency describes all the services that it provides its clientele and allows them to select the service they think best suits their needs. If it turns out that the person has not made a wise choice, then they discuss their options with their therapist. This approach is based on the idea, central to SST, that the client, given sufficient information, can decide what is best for them. It is the same assumption that underpins single-session walk-in therapy. Here, clients are trusted to make decisions that are in their best interests.

The Person Is Selected for SST

A second way of approaching the same question is for an intake worker at the agency to which the person has applied for help to interview the person when they first seek help to determine which of the agency's services is right for the person. While the person may be asked for their opinion on the matter, the intake worker takes upon themself the bulk of the responsibility in deciding on the service to which the person is best suited. To facilitate the work of such intake workers, the agency provides them with inclusion and exclusion criteria to help them make a decision that they think is in the person's best interests.

Of all the approaches to help the person access SST, this one is the least compatible with single-session thinking (see *Principle 3*). First, it places the responsibility for such decision-making mainly with the agency's intake worker and not with the person themself. Second, it goes against the SST view that the best way of finding out if a person will benefit from single-session therapy is to give them a single session and see if they benefit from it. Third, the agency's time in determining whether or not the person is suited to SST could be better spent offering them SST.

The Person is Offered SST as a Matter of Course

Some agencies organise their services so that everybody is seen for a single session, at the end of which they are given a choice. First, they can determine whether they want further help. Or, second, they can opt to go away, reflect on the session, digest what they have learned, take appropriate action, let time pass and decide at that point what they want to do vis-à-vis further help. This approach to offering SST is based on research that has shown that:

- The modal[7] number of sessions clients have is one, followed by two, followed by three, etc.
- 70–80 per cent of these clients are satisfied with the single session given their circumstances
- Therapists do not know which clients will have one session and which will have more (Hoyt and Talmon, 2014a; Young, 2018).

When this approach is taken, then 50 per cent of clients require no further help. As noted above, we do not know which clients will opt to have more help and which will not.

From Helping-Seeking to the Session

We know very little about the factors that lead a person to decide to seek therapeutic help and how they end up at a walk-in centre or at a clinic that offers SST seeking this form of help. For the present discussion, I define help-seeking as the moment that a person walks into a walk-in centre or the moment that they contact an agency that offers SST as one of their services.

---

[7] The mode is the most frequently occurring number in a series.

After the Person Walks-in and Before They See a Therapist

Although the idea of a walk-in centre is that a person accesses help straightaway, in practice, there is a short wait before a therapist sees the person. During that time, the person can be asked to complete a brief intake form and, more importantly, a form to help them prepare for the session. It is best if the receptionist gives the person a rationale for completing the preparation form, stressing that doing so will help both the person and their therapist prepare for the session. However, it is also important for the receptionist to stress that completing the preparation form is optional. Given the importance of the client preparing for the session, I suggest that receptionists are trained to present this rationale to people turning up to the walk-in centre.

After the Person Contacts an Agency for an Appointment and Before They See a Therapist

I discussed earlier in this principle what happens before a decision has been made (either by the client themself or an intake worker) that the person will access SST in a multi-service agency. Once that decision has been made, it is important that the person sees a therapist as quickly as possible and is also asked to prepare for the session. In my experience, when the therapist contacts the client directly to introduce themself and asks the client to complete a pre-session preparation form, having given them a rationale to do so, and asks them to return it so that they can also prepare for the session, then this increases the chances that the client will engage with the task. However, if an intake worker asks them to do so and sends them a pre-session preparation form and other forms and question-naires to complete, this decreases the chances that they will engage with the task.

An example of a pre-session preparation questionnaire that I use in my SST practice is presented in Appendix 3.

In SST by appointment, what is particularly important is that the time between the appointment being made and it taking place is (a) as short as possible and (b) used well.

My view is that an agency should provide a client with an SST appointment between two and three days after contacting that agency for help. Anything more than a week's wait tends to be inconsistent with the 'help provided at the point of need' perspective that underpins SST.

More Help Is Available

I have already made the point that SST as a service delivery mode sits alongside other services offered by an agency. In *Principle 1,* I also stressed that the therapist needs to be transparent both about the nature of SST and what help is available to the client should they need it. If the person decides to seek further help either at the end of the single session or later (e.g. when the therapist follows-up the client to see if they need further help), and the agency offers such help, then the therapist explains the access process and how long the waiting period is. If the agency does not provide the service that the client requires, then plausible alternatives are discussed.

*

In the next principle, I will discuss single-session thinking or what some refer to as the single-session mindset. This mindset underpins good practice in SST, as I will discuss later in *Principle 6*. By contrast, if a therapist tries to practise SST without being informed by single-session thinking, they will experience many roadblocks to effective SST practice.

PRINCIPLE 3

Adopting the Single-Session Mindset

It is challenging to practise single-session therapy well if a therapist brings a conventional therapy mindset to the work rather than a single-session mindset or what is currently known as single-session thinking (Hoyt, Young and Rycroft, 2020).[8] In this principle, I will outline the elements of the single-session mindset and compare these, when appropriate, with the conventional therapy mindset. In *Principle 6*, I will focus on the practice that stems from the single-session mindset.

Respond Quickly

A central feature of single-session therapy is that the therapist holds in mind the importance of providing a quick response to a client who comes forward for help. There are three aspects of this rapid response that characterise the single-session mindset: prompt accessibility, developing a working alliance quickly and the immediate provision of therapy.

---

[8] I will use these terms interchangeably in this book.

Prompt Accessibility

As discussed in *Principle 2,* the context of SST is vital to the practice of this mode of service delivery. It is central to the way therapists think about SST that it is made accessible to clients in a prompt manner. This is most evident in walk-in centres where clients can get access to an hour of therapy focused on their stated wants almost immediately. It is also important in agencies that offer SST by appointment. As I argued in the previous principle such agencies should aim to provide SST to those wishing to avail themselves of it within 2/3 days from when they apply for such help. When there are barriers to such prompt accessibility, it tends to stem from agencies applying conventional thinking to SST provision, such as assessing a client's suitability for SST. Applying SST thinking to SST provision is vital if such barriers are to be removed to prompt accessibility.

Developing a Working Alliance Quickly

The second feature of providing a quick response to therapy within the SST mindset also runs counter to conventional thinking. In the latter mindset, while a working alliance is deemed central to the effectiveness of therapeutic work, it is generally agreed that such an alliance between the therapist and the client takes time to develop and certainly requires more than one session. By contrast, SST therapists do think that they can create a working alliance quickly, and in *Principle 5*, I will discuss how this can be done. Indeed, research shows that the working alliance is an important determinant in explaining who benefits from a single session and who does not (Simon, Imel, Ludman, and Steinfeld (2012).

Immediate Therapy

As I will discuss later in this principle, the third feature of the 'respond quickly' part of the single-session mindset is using time well by providing therapy at the outset.

The Importance of Being Transparent

The single-session therapist keeps in mind throughout the session the importance of being transparent. This explains why they ask the client at the outset to share what their expectations are from the session. In response, if necessary, the therapist is prepared to say what they can do and what they can't do in SST. They are also transparent about what help is available to the client if they need further therapy and how long they will have to wait for such assistance. Finally, the therapist is open, if asked, about their view of the client's problem and what might constitute a viable solution.

Approaching the Session

The SST practitioner approaches the session with the idea that this could be the only session they will have with the client. This may be the case irrespective of the client's diagnosis or the severity or complexity of their problem. In conventional thinking, the more severe or complex the client's issues, the longer the therapy should be, in the therapist's view.

I have a colleague whose view is that the purpose of the first session in psychotherapy is to get the client to come back for a second session. This is very much an example of conventional thinking and is in stark contrast with single-session thinking, where the purpose of the first session is to work effectively with the client so that they do not need another session but that they can have one if required.

Another critical feature of single-session thinking that is uppermost in the therapist's mind as they approach the session is that they view the session as a whole, complete in itself. As I will discuss in the next principle, this means conceptualising the session as having its own process with a beginning, a middle and an end (Hoyt, 2000, 2018). Therapists who approach the session with conventional thinking are generally worried about how they can 'squeeze' everything they need to do into a single session and are always looking for ways to offer clients more sessions whether they ask for additional help or not.

The Power of Now and Making Use of the Time Available

Whenever I give a workshop on 'Single-Session Therapy', I ask participants how they know for sure that the client they have before them for a first session will return for a second. Participants admit that they don't know this. Single-session therapists take the view that since it may well be the case that the person will not return for a second session (although, of course, they may), then they will use the 'power of now' to help them in the moment, making use of all the time that is available to them both. I often do SST demonstrations, the average time being about 20 minutes (Dryden, 2018) and have usually found that the client can derive something meaningful even from such a brief session. Therapists who think conventionally would blanch if they were only given 20 minutes to help someone! Appelbaum (1975) referred to this as 'Parkinson's Law of Psychotherapy', where therapy takes as much time as you allocate to it.

The Client Decides What They Want, Not What the Therapist Thinks They Need

In conventional thinking, the therapist is interested in what the client wants from therapy, but by this, they mean at therapy's end rather than at the end of the session. When thinking conventionally, the therapist is particularly interested in the complete clinical picture concerning what problems the client has, how severe and complex these problems are and, in some cases, what the client's diagnosis is. From all this information, the therapist comes to a judgement concerning what the client needs from therapy. The single-session therapist is far less interested in these matters because they are concerned about helping the client leave the session satisfied that they have gotten what they came for. They are focused on what the client wants and not on the conventional view of what the client may need.

The Clients Decides How Much Help They Want

The single-session therapist is aware of the research that shows that the modal number of session clients have is 'one' and that they are mostly satisfied with this session (Hoyt and Talmon, 2014a). In commenting on their research that demonstrated the same finding, Brown and Jones (2005) said that this suggests that the client rather than the therapist determines therapy length. Conventional thinking leads the therapist to think that they should determine how long the client needs to come for based on their assessment of the client and on a case history. However, the single-session therapist agrees with Hoyt, Young and Rycroft (2020: 224), who say that 'clients are far less interested in psychotherapy than are therapists and prefer brief therapeutic encounters'.

Do Not Spend Time on Assessment of Client Suitability for SST

When I first became interested in single-session therapy, I brought my conventional clinical thinking to the question of client suitability. Thus, I developed a long list of client indications and contra-indications for SST. Then, I realised that I was planning to use valuable therapeutic time to determine which clients will benefit from SST and which clients won't, rather than spending that time doing therapy with a client, a practice consistent with the single-session mindset. Single-session thinking holds that the only way to discover whether a client will benefit from SST is to give them a single session and see if they benefit from it. Therapists are not good at making such determinations in advance.

The idea that no client suitability assessment is needed mainly comes from single-session walk-in therapy. Anyone can walk into a walk-in centre for a single therapy session irrespective of their diagnosis and how serious or complex their problems are. There are no attempts to determine a client's suitability for single-session walk-in therapy, and this approach permeates single-session thinking.

Plan to Start Therapy from Moment One

Another critical aspect of single-session thinking also comes from walk-in therapy. It is that the therapist has it in mind to begin therapy from moment one. This is very much at odds with conventional thinking, which recommends that the therapist starts work with a client by undertaking such activities as client assessment, case history-taking and case formulation. When sufficient information has been gained from these activities, then therapy commences.

Strengths and Resources Are More Useful than Deficits

We have seen that the single-session therapist has it in mind that as they may only be seeing the client once, therapy begins from moment one. As such, there is more to be gained by the therapist identifying and utilising a client's strengths and the resources available to them in their environment than by focusing on their deficits and weaknesses.

Meeting the Client's Preferences for Being Helped, If Possible

The therapist recognises that different clients may seek various types of help from SST. As such, the therapist seeks to understand what kind of service the client is seeking and endeavours to meet these treatment preferences unless there is a good reason not to do so (Norcross and Cooper, 2021). Perhaps the most common form of help that a client wants from SST is emotional problem-solving. However, some clients want an opportunity to explore a concern, time to express their feelings about an issue, help to make a decision or assistance to resolve a dilemma. These different types of helping require the therapist to be flexible in their SST practice, a topic I discuss more fully in *Principles 6* and *7*.

Agreeing on a Focus and Keeping to It

When a therapist holds a conventional therapy mindset, once they initiate therapy (after assessment, history-taking etc.), they will encourage the client to talk in their own way about why they have come to therapy and what they want to gain from it. Some therapists regard this as following the client's 'process' and are reluctant to intervene much at the outset. In the vast majority of cases, this type of thinking will not lead to productive use of a single session.

Unless a client has said that the best way for them to use the session is to 'roam free' by talking about anything they want to, then the therapist is guided by single-session thinking that states that the best way for the therapeutic dyad to use the time available to them is for the therapist to agree on a focus for the session with the client. A focus may be dictated by the client's problem, goal, or search for a solution to their problem.

Sometimes the therapist will offer a structure for the session, which determines a focus for the client. For example, the therapist may think that the purpose of SST is to help the client deal with their 'most pressing concern' and will use this language when assisting the client in creating a productive focus. For me, this is too limiting because the person may wish to discuss a different issue to their most pressing concern and may not feel able to do so if I ask for the latter. My mindset is that I will be guided by the client's response to my opening question: 'What is your understanding of the purpose of our conversation today' and proceed from there in helping the client create an agreed focus.

Once the therapist and client have agreed on a focus, the therapist has two points in mind. First, the therapist needs to check periodically that the focus is what the person wants to discuss because sometimes it isn't. In this case, a change in focus needs to be made. Second, the therapist needs to intervene to help the client keep to the focus if they drift away from it. Unless helped to keep to a focus, a client may naturally move away from it and go on to discuss one or more different topics. This is natural in everyday conversation, but a single-session conversation is different. As such, in my view, it is the therapist's responsibility to help the client maintain the agreed focus, not the client's.

Working Together to Find a Solution

When the client is looking for a solution to a nominated problem, the therapist has it in mind to help the client draw from several sources. These include: (1) what the client has found helpful in addressing the problem in the past and what they have found helpful in addressing other issues; (2) constructive alternatives to forms of thinking and behaviour that maintain their problem; (3) the strengths that the client has that may contribute to a solution to their nominated problem; (4) other people who may similarly contribute; (5) ideas that the client has that may contribute to a solution; and (6) ideas that the therapist has that may similarly contribute.

Experience Ignites Discussion, Planning Capitalises on Experience

Suppose the therapist and client have co-created a solution to the client's problem. In that case, the therapist has it in mind to suggest to the client that they gain some in-session experience of the solution, if possible, before helping them to formulate a plan to implement this solution in their everyday life.

Asking the Client to Summarise the Work

In line with the principle that the client needs to be an active collaborator with the therapist in the session, the therapist has it in mind to ask the client to summarise the work they have done together in the session. I tend to do this both halfway through the session and also at the end. Conventional thinking suggests that the therapist should summarise. However, the single-session therapist wants the client to take away their own summary rather than the therapist's summary since they will be more influenced in practice by the former than the latter, in general.

Encouraging the Client to Take Away at Least One Thing

After the client has summarised the work they and the therapist have done together, the therapist encourages the client to take away at least one thing that can make a difference to them in their life going forward and, as suggested earlier, a plan to implement this. Of course, the client may take away more than one thing from the session, but this is their choice. The therapist should refrain from offering them more than they wish to takeaway. By contrast, therapists who bring conventional thinking to SST often think of all the things they want the client to take away from the session when there is a good chance that they will not return. When they operationalise this mindset, they tend to overload and overwhelm the client, who is in danger of taking away nothing when this 'overegging the pudding' approach is taken.

All's Well that End's Well

Jerome Frank (1961), in the first edition of his classic text, *Persuasion and Healing*, argued that although clients come for therapy with a myriad of different symptoms, the unifying factor beneath such help-seeking is that they are in a state of demoralisation. The purpose of therapy, therefore, is to help restore the client's morale. This is what the single-session therapist aims to do by the end of the session. Thus, it is so important for the session to come to a satisfactory conclusion. This helps the client to look forward to the future with some degree of hope based on the work that they have done with their therapist and knowing that more help is available if needed. I discuss how the SST practitioner implements this aspect of single-session thinking in *Principle 6*.

The Importance of Multiple Mindsets in Psychotherapy

While I have concentrated on the topic of the single-session mindset in this principle and contrasted it with a more conventional therapeutic mindset, I want to close by saying that it is important that the therapist becomes comfortable in working from multiple mindsets and competent at applying whichever mindset best suits the work that they are currently doing. Thus, while there is nothing inherently wrong with a conventional therapy mindset, it just does not fit the practical requirements of single-session work.

*

In the following principle, I present the idea that SST is a process with a preparation period, a beginning, a middle, an end and a follow-up phase.

PRINCIPLE 4

Thinking of Single-Session Therapy as a Process

I mentioned in *Principle 3* that SST practitioners tend to think of the session in single-session therapy as complete in itself. However, as noted in *Principle 1,* more help is available in SST. So, there is more to SST than the single session that appears in the name of this mode of service delivery. In this principle, I will consider SST as a process that begins before the therapist and client meet and ends with the therapist following-up with the client to see how they are getting on and if they need further therapeutic help (Hoyt, 2000, 2018). This process has six phases:

1. Before the person and therapist agree to work together in SST
2. The pre-session preparation phase
3. The early phase of the session
4. The middle phase of the session
5. The late phase of the session
6. The follow-through phase

The competent SST practitioner keeps these phases in mind while working with the client before, during and after the session. Also, I will discuss the issue concerning *when* a person becomes an SST client because there is no agreed position on this issue.

Phase 1: Before the Person and Therapist Agree to Work Together in SST

While it may be thought that the process of SST begins when the client and therapist first meet one another, there is a case for viewing the first phase of SST as commencing before the therapist and client decide to work together in an SST context.[9] This view which derives from American interpersonal social work (Garvin and Seabury, 1997) and developed by me (Dryden, 2019a), states that a person can occupy several help-seeking roles before becoming an SST client. These three roles are (1) the explorer role, (2) the enquirer role, and (3) the applicant role.

The Explorer Role

When a person occupies the 'explorer' role, they are considering seeking therapeutic help but unsure

---

[9] In this principle, I will outline the process of SST by appointment rather than by walk-in since the former is more common in the UK than the latter.

what will help them. Concerning SST, the person may be wondering which mode of therapy service delivery to access and are exploring these different modes, including SST. A defining feature of the person who occupies the explorer role is that they do not directly contact a therapist or therapy agency. They may gain information from consulting various websites or from several relevant people, including clients of these services. As a result of their exploration, they may decide that they wish to seek SST, and consequently, they narrow their search to agencies and/or therapists who offer SST. During their more detailed exploration, they may discover particular agencies or practitioners that capture their interest. As a result, they decide to make some enquiries of one or more of these agencies or practitioners.

The Enquirer Role

When the person occupies the 'enquirer' role, they have concluded, as stated above, that SST might help them and have begun to make enquiries of particular agencies or practitioners who offer SST. The person may ask a range of questions. They may request more detailed information than is provided on the agency's or practitioner's website. Thus, they may ask about how to access SST if this is not clear, what the fees are and how long they will have to wait to be seen.

My own experience is that people may bypass the explorer role and go straight to the enquirer role. Thus, people find out that I offer SST and contact me directly to ask me about SST, what it is and whether it will benefit them. If their enquiry is focused, I am happy to answer specific questions, usually over the telephone or by email. However, if their queries are general, I offer to send them a leaflet that I have specially written for potential clients (see Appendix 1). I may also direct them to the SST whiteboard animation that I have developed (see https://www. youtube.com/watch?v=wIcuOVOABRw).[10] the text of which appears in Appendix 2).

The Applicant Role

When the person occupies the 'applicant' role, they have decided that they want to avail themself of SST and have selected an agency or therapist they think may be best able to help them. Consequently, the person makes contact with the agency or practitioner that they believe is best suited to them to make an appointment. In other words, the person has made an application for single-session help from their selected agency or therapist.

---

[10] Accessed on 12 February 2021.

When Does the Person Become a Client?

So far in the process, the person has not yet become a client and strangely enough, while it is clear that a person becomes an SST client when both they and their client have given informed consent to proceed, there is no agreed point in SST when such 'clienthood' is achieved.

In part, this depends on who the person has been speaking to when they have made an application to become an SST client. Let's first take the case when the person approaches an agency that offers SST and speaks to an intake worker. Suppose that the worker has explained the nature of SST and such matters as the agency's confidentiality policy, fees, and cancellation policy accurately. In that case, the applicant becomes a client, *from their perspective*, when they have agreed to these matters. At this point, they are asked to prepare for the session (see below). However, it is important to be aware that they have not yet met the therapist. According to the point made above, the person *actually* becomes a client when they and their therapist have both given their informed consent to proceed. Thus, it may be when the therapist and client meet for the first time that it is clear that the person wants a different service than SST. In which case, the therapist will not give their informed consent to SST, and the pair negotiate consent to a different service.

Second, let's consider the case when the intake worker does not explain the nature of SST directly and/or has not outlined the agency's policy on confidentiality, fees and cancellation period. In this case, the person is asked to complete the pre-session preparation form without becoming a client. They become a client when all these matters are explained to them by the therapist at the beginning of the session, and then both give their informed consent to proceed based on the outcome of the ensuing discussion.

Finally, let's consider when the person applies for SST help directly from a therapist who offers SST as part of their service delivery. Here, the therapist talks to the person directly when they are in the applicant role and can thus explain SST themself and clarify their policies on confidentiality, fees, and cancellation period. When both agree to go forward, the client becomes a client of the process before they complete the pre-session questionnaire.

Phase 2: The Pre-Session Preparation Phase

As noted in *Principle 1*, some therapists in the single-session therapy community consider that SST comprises only a single session – no pre-session preparation or follow-up. However, this is a minority view, and many SST practitioners who offer SST by appointment do include both of these facilities.

As I discussed in *Principle 3*, the productive use of time in SST is a vital part of single-session thinking. Thus, in SST by appointment, once the person has been given a date for their single session, they can be asked to use the time between the appointment being arranged and the session by preparing for the session. This can either be done by telephone or by questionnaire (see Dryden, 2017 and Appendix 3). While this is predominantly to help the person prepare so that they can get the most from the session, it also helps the therapist prepare for the session. Such pre-session contact can also help induct the person into SST and plant the seeds for change.

When the person has applied to an agency and is asked to complete a pre-session preparation questionnaire by the intake worker, they are more likely to fully do so when they receive a good rationale for its completion. However, this does not always happen with the result that the person does not complete the questionnaire at all or does so in a cursory manner.

In my view, good practice occurs in agencies when the therapist emails the client directly to introduce themself to the client, as discussed in *Principle 2*. In doing so, the therapist attaches the questionnaire and provides the person with a plausible rationale for its completion. When this happens, it increases the chances that the person will engage fully with this task. They are then asked to return the completed questionnaire to the therapist before the session. When this occurs, and when both the person and the therapist are prepared for the session, the client usually gets more from the session than when this does not happen.

When the person has applied to an independent practitioner, they can choose to have the pre-session preparation contact by telephone or by questionnaire. As they are in direct contact with the therapist they will see for SST, they are likely to engage with the preparation task fully. This happens because the therapist will ensure they do so when the preparation is done by phone and will provide a plausible rationale for completion of the question-naire when this is the selected form of preparation.

Phase 3: The Early Phase of the Session

We have now reached the stage where the client and therapist meet for their session. The therapist begins the session by clarifying the purpose of their meeting with the client and explaining how they can access further help if needed. If not already done, the therapist describes their or the agency's confidentiality policies, the payment of fees, and the cancellation period if the person requests further help. Again, if not already done, the client and therapist both give their informed consent to proceed.

If the person has prepared for the session, the therapist asks if the client has experienced any change on the issue for which they seek help and if so, the therapist will capitalise on this change. In this early phase of the session, the therapist sets out to form a productive working alliance with the client and demonstrates their keenness to help the client as quickly as possible (see *Principle 5* for a full discussion of the working alliance in SST). Perhaps the most crucial task that the therapist has in the early phase of the session is to discover what the person wants help with and agree on a focus for the session, reflecting the issue/concern/problem that the person has nominated. Within this focus, the therapist encourages the client to identify a goal for the session and helps the client to maintain this focus throughout the session.

Phase 4: The Middle Phase of the Session

In the middle phase of the session, the therapist works with the client to identify a solution to the client's nominated problem. This involves looking for something that the client can change that is centrally implicated in the issue. For example, this may be a mechanism that is responsible for the maintenance of the problem, which, if modified, would help the client solve their problem. From a working alliance perspective, it is important for the therapist and client to agree on what this mechanism is and that it should be the target for change (Dryden, 2011). How the client can change this mechanism depends on several factors. First, it depends on the client's view of how this factor can be best changed and to what it needs to be changed. Second, it depends on what the client has tried before concerning effecting such change, what has worked and what has not. Third, it depends on what inner strengths and external resources the client can make use of during the change process. Finally, it depends on what orientation-specific concepts the therapist introduces into the change-related discussion. On this point, it is best if the therapist has asked the client if they are interested in the therapist's perspective on this issue before the therapist introduces it.

The agreed solution emerges from a discussion of all these points. Then, the client and therapist discuss the practicality of the solution and its likely effectiveness in effecting the desired change. It is important to note here that the most effective solution may not be the most practicable. Thus, the therapist should preferably help the client select a solution that they will implement even if it is less therapeutically powerful than another solution that the client may not execute.

Once a solution has been agreed upon, the therapist suggests, if practicable, that the client rehearses the solution in the session to get some experience in implementing it. If the client concludes that the solution is not right for them based on this experience, then another solution is selected and rehearsed. However, if the client concludes that the first solution is right for them, they still can make some changes to the solution, if necessary.

Phase 5: The Late Phase of the Session

In the late SST phase, the therapist and client discuss how they can implement the agreed solution they have selected and rehearsed earlier in the session (Hoyt and Rosenbaum, 2018). This is centred on action planning, where the client decides on a *broad* strategy of implementation. While specific examples of such action planning may be identified, mainly to help the client to 'kick start' the process, the emphasis is on one primary broad implementation principle. When this has been done, the therapist can then ask the client to identify and problem-solve any obstacles to implementing their action plan.

Also, in this late phase, the therapist can ask the client to summarise what they learned from the session and what they will take away with them. As mentioned in *Principle 3*, it is more valuable for the client to summarise than it is for the therapist to do so. The therapist's summary may stress different things than the client's summary and may lead the client to take away what the therapist thinks the client has learned rather than what the client has actually learned. It may be that when the client has summarised the work, the solution that was identified in the middle phase of the session is different from the client's takeaway. If this happens, the therapist should find ways of linking the client's solution and the client's takeaway so that they can be integrated. If not, the client should be asked to prioritise the one over the other if they are different.

Once this has been done, the therapist can begin to wrap things up. During this part of the process, the therapist should encourage the client to ask any last-minute questions related to the issue at hand and/or make any final points again related to the discussed issue. Then, the therapist plans for a follow-up with the client, who should also be reminded that they can access help in the future should they need to and how this can be done.

The purpose of this late phase is for the client to leave the session on a good note and optimistic that they can operationalise meaningful learning from the session.

Phase 6: The Follow-Through Phase

The follow-through phase involves the client being followed up by the therapist (or an agency representative) at an agreed date following the session. The purpose of this follow-up is two-fold. First, it is to discover the client's longer-term outcome (outcome evaluation) and second, to find out from the client what they thought about the service they received (service evaluation). This is a good time for the client to be asked again if they need further help if they have not already requested it or indicate they do not require such help.

*

One of the most common questions about SST is how a therapist can develop an effective working relationship with a client in this mode of service delivery. In the following principle, I will show how this can be done by using Bordin's (1979) tripartite model of the working alliance, together with my later addition (Dryden, 2011).

PRINCIPLE 5

Developing the Working Alliance Quickly in SST

Therapists new to single-session therapy often have an ambivalent attitude to this way of working. On the one hand, they are attracted to the idea of helping people quickly, on the other hand, they are doubtful whether it is possible to develop a working relationship in such a brief period. Indeed, the view that psychotherapy needs more than one session for a relationship to develop formed the basis of a legal case in Ontario, Canada. In 2016, the newly formed College of Registered Psychotherapists of Ontario (CRPO) decided that SST was not psychotherapy. Thus, SST hours could not count towards a person gaining access to the CRPO register through the grandparenting route. Their reasoning was as follows. The presence of a therapeutic relationship characterises psychotherapy, and such a relationship can only develop over time. Therefore, as a therapeutic relationship cannot develop in single-session therapy, SST is not psychotherapy. This was challenged in the courts, and the CRPO's decision was eventually overturned. Karen Young, a Canadian single-session therapist, was used as an expert witness during the appeal and presented a wealth of evidence to show that a therapeutic relationship can indeed be established in SST (see Young and Jebreen, 2019). For example, 344 SST clients completed the Session Rating Scale (SRS) at the end of their session, and results showed that clients and therapists could have a strong working alliance in the session (Young and Bhanot-Malhotra. 2014). In addition, although not mentioned by Young and Jebreen (2019), a study by Simon, Imel, Ludman and Steinfeld (2012) showed that clients who developed a positive working alliance with their therapists in SST had a better outcome than clients who did not forge such a relationship with their practitioners. Thus, a good working alliance can be developed in SST and in the rest of this principle, I will use my updated version of Ed Bordin's (1979) framework to show how (Dryden, 2011).

According to Bordin (1979), the working alliance comprises three components: bonds, goals and tasks. Later, I added a fourth component, views (Dryden, 2011).

Bonds

The bond refers to the interpersonal connectedness between therapist and client. From the perspective of what is commonly known as the 'core therapeutic conditions' (Rogers, 1957), it is vital that the client experiences the therapist as empathic, unconditionally accepting and transparent.

Empathy

At the early phase of the SST session, the therapist asks the client to nominate an issue/concern/or problem that will become the session's focus. When the client does so and explains the nature of this issue, for example, then it is important that the therapist conveys their understanding of this issue from the client's frame of reference. As the two proceed, it is again important for the therapist to express their understanding of the client's struggle in living with this issue.

Unconditional acceptance

Quite often, a client in SST will disclose a self-critical attitude. In response, the therapist should demonstrate an attitude of unconditional acceptance of the client and, if appropriate, to encourage the client to begin to show themself the same attitude.

Transparency

In *Principle 3*. I argued that being prepared to be transparent is an important aspect of single-session thinking. It is also an important part of developing a good working alliance. Thus, as mentioned before, the therapist needs to make explicit what they can do in SST and what they can't do if this becomes appropriate.

Nowhere is transparency more prevalent than in Young's 'No Bullshit Therapy' – NBT (see Findlay, 2007). Here is what Young (2018: 55) says about his approach. 'NBT is enacted by creating a context where a therapist (and client) can be honest and direct, where the therapist can challenge from a good and caring place, can marry honesty and directness with warmth and care, and promote transparency and reduce obfuscation by avoiding jargon.... Creating transparency in keeping with the philosophy of SST with mandated clients may look like stating how you prefer to work and seeking the client's response ("I like to be pretty upfront and direct; how does that fit with you?"), rather than making the assumption that the client wants to collaborate with you.'

Other Aspects of the Bond

In addition to the 'core therapeutic conditions', there are other aspects of the bond relevant to SST.

The therapist's eagerness to help: One of the therapist qualities that, in my view, strengthens the therapeutic bond is their eagerness to help the client in the session that they are currently having. The therapist demonstrates this by getting down to business immediately and helping the two of them keep to an agreed focus once one has been created.

Collaboration: Clients who have chosen to seek single-session therapy will be invited to collaborate with their therapist. The collaborative bond involves the following features:

- It is largely client-directed, with the therapist sharing any concerns that they may have about the client's chosen direction.
- There is explicit negotiation between the therapist and the concerning what should be the focus of the work and what are realistic goals.
- The therapist and client work together to find a solution to the client's problem.
- SST is a fusion between what the client brings to the process and what the therapist brings to the process. The therapist can share their expertise, when needed, without adopting the role of the 'expert'.
- The therapist and client discuss whether further help is needed and if so, they agree on a pathway towards such help.
- The therapist and client decide together on follow-up – if it is to occur and, if so, when.

Views

The 'views' component of the working alliance is the one that I introduced (see Dryden, 2011) and concerns the understandings that both participants hold about salient aspects of the SST process. The critical point about these understandings is that the therapist and client end up agreeing on their respective views even if they may hold different understandings at the outset.

In my opinion, there are three main areas where client and therapist need to have such an agreement.

Views on SST

In my opinion, it is vital that the client and therapist agree on the nature of SST, as discussed in *Principle 1*. Does it mean only one session and one session only or can the client have further sessions if they want to? If they request and are offered further help are these sessions booked one at a time (as in One-At-A-Time therapy), or can the client book for a series of sessions? (Dryden, 2019b).

Views on the Problem and What Accounts for It

When an SST practitioner works with a client's problem, it is vital that they have an agreed understanding of this problem and what factors explain its existence. This is the case if the therapist shares their professional understanding of the client's problem or whether the therapist elicits the client's view on the same problem. If they do not share a negotiated view of the problem, they may end up working at cross-purposes.

Views on How the Problem Can Be Best Addressed

It is also vital that the client and therapist have a shared understanding of how the client's nominated problem can best be tackled. If not, they will again be working at cross-purposes, and the client will not get as much from the session as they could. When solutions are discussed, it is crucial that the eventually agreed solution is negotiated and that both can see that it has the potency to help the client to achieve their goal, if implemented.

In family-oriented SST, the sessions are often watched by an auxiliary observing team whose primary purpose is to arrive at a solution that the family is likely to implement, helping them achieve their goals. The primary therapist or therapy team takes a mid-session break to meet with the observing team. Here, if such a solution is to 'work', all three parties need to agree on this point. In the interests of transparency, it is best if the therapy and observing teams include the family in their discussion about solutions and that all three have input into the selected solution.

Goals

In this section, I will discuss the client's goals and the therapist's goals in SST.

The Client's Goals

All therapy is purposive, and this is especially the case with SST. What is specific to SST concerning goals is that the client is asked to specify a goal for the end of the session (e.g. 'If, at the end of the session, you thought that you got what you were hoping for, what would that be?') rather than a goal for the end of treatment that is deemed to last longer than one session. Both sets of goals are outcome related. In SST, it is probably better for specific goals to be negotiated than general ones. However, if the latter is agreed upon, it is paramount that both client and therapist are clear about how they will both know if these are achieved. However, it is useful to recognise that in SST, the therapist will, in most cases, not know if the client has achieved their goal if and until a follow-up session is carried out.

The critical point about goals from a working alliance perspective is that the client and therapist agree on the client's goals so that they can work together to achieve them. If not, the single session has the quality of the client resisting the therapist's efforts to take them in a direction to which they have not agreed, however 'healthy' such a goal may be.

Sometimes when a client sets what at first sight is an outcome goal, it is actually a process goal. Thus a client might say that they are looking for some insight or some understanding into a problem. I regard this as a process goal. When this happens, I generally ask something like, 'If you got the insight or understanding that you are looking for, what would you do with it?' This usually leads to an outcome goal.

The Therapist's Goals

From the therapist's perspective, some of their goals are related to the client's outcome, while others are related to process issues.

The therapist's goals related to client outcome: The following are common therapist goals concerning client outcome:

- *To help the client achieve their session goal:* Given the fact that the client may only come for one session, it makes sense that the therapist would set as their goal to help the client achieve their session goal.
- *To help the client get 'unstuck':* Quite often, a client reports being stuck with an issue, and it is a legitimate goal for the therapist to help the client get 'unstuck'.

- *To help the client take a few steps forward which may help them to travel the rest of the journey without professional assistance:* This point is based on Lao Tzu's words, 'The journey of a thousand miles begins with one step.'

The therapist's goals concerning process issues: The following are common therapist process goals. The achievement of these process goals is, of course, in the service of helping the client to achieve their outcome goals.

- *To help the client address a specific issue:* Frequently, the client comes to SST hoping to address a specific issue and here, the therapist's goal is to help them to do just that.
- *To give the client space and opportunity to think and explore when needed:* Less commonly, the client comes to SST wishing to explore a particular issue. This is a legitimate way of using a single session, and the therapist should set themself the goal to help the client do this.
- *To help the client see that they have the resources to achieve their goals:* Since time is limited in SST, the therapist does not have time to teach the client skills that they do not have in their repertoire that might help address their problem. A better use of such time and a valid

process goal is for the therapist to help the client see that they may already have the internal and external resources to deal with their nominated issue.

- *To help the client select a possible solution:* I define a 'solution' as something that enables the person to address their concern effectively and thereby achieve their goal. When the client seeks a solution, the goal of the SST practitioner should be to help them do this.

- *To give the client the experience of the solution in the session, if possible:* A client is more likely to implement a solution that they have had an opportunity to rehearse than when they have not had such an opportunity. Therefore, it is a useful process goal for the therapist to help the client to practise a solution, if relevant and practicable

- *To help the client develop an action plan:* Similarly, a client is more likely to implement a selected solution if they have developed a plan to do this than if they haven't. Consequently, another process goal is for the therapist to facilitates such action planning.

Tasks

Tasks are activities carried out by both client and therapist that are in the service of the client's goals. I will discuss the single-session therapist's tasks in detail in *Principle 6*. From a working alliance perspective, it is vital for the client and therapist to understand one another's tasks, and agree, either explicitly or implicitly, that the execution of these tasks is a useful way forward.

The Alliance Is with the Agency, Not with Any Particular Therapist

In a single-session walk-in therapy centre, most clients do not walk back in for another session, although a minority of them do. This latter group is not put off by the fact that they do not know who will be on duty when they walk-in for a subsequent session, and therefore it is likely that they will see a different therapist to the one they initially saw. This does not appear to deter them from using the services of the walk-in centre.

When a UK university introduced a 'one-at-a-time' mode of counselling delivery where students could only book one session at a time, a student who wanted a subsequent session could opt to see their original counsellor or a new counsellor. About 40 per cent of returning students chose to see a new counsellor stating that they would value a new perspective on their issue.

These two scenarios imply that in single-session work, clients tend to see that they have an alliance with the agency that offers such work rather than with any particular therapist who works in this agency. Given the practical difficulties of arranging continuity of therapy for single-session clients, I consider that this is an encouraging finding.

*

In the next two principles, I discuss implementing good practice in SST. In *Principle 6,* I focus on what the single-session community, as a whole, considers to be good practice and how the SST practitioner can implement such practice.

PRINCIPLE 6

Implementing Good Practice in SST: I. Consensual Contributions

One of the first publications on single-session therapy that helped to define the field was written by Bernard Bloom (1981). In that publication, Bloom outlined several therapeutic factors that characterised his focused approach to SST (see Dryden, 2019a, for further information). This chapter was followed by Moshe Talmon's (1990) book, *Single Session Therapy: Maximising the Effect of the First (and Often Only) Therapeutic Encounter.* In this text, Talmon outlined further ways of practising SST. Additional publications contributed to this work (Hoyt and Talmon, 2014b, Hoyt, Bobele, Slive, Young and Talmon, 2018). This cadre of work has led to a consensual view of good practice in SST, which I will outline and discuss in this principle. However, it is important to note that a consensual view of such good practice does not mean that there is no place for idiosyncratic and creative contributions. Far from it, and I will discuss the place of such contributions in *Principle 7.*

Consensual Contributions to Good SST Practice

The following points are considered to be good practice in SST. I see these points to be akin to tools in the toolbox of a handyperson. Not all tools are used in every session, but they are in the toolbox should they be required. While the following will emphasise the strategic and technical aspects of SST, please do not forget the message of *Principle 5*: the practice of effective single-session therapy occurs within the context of a good working alliance between therapist and client (Simon et al., 2012).

- *The therapist forms an agreement with the client concerning the purpose of the session and what can and cannot be achieved*

  When the therapist meets the client for the session, they assume that this may be the last time that they will be meeting, while at the same time being open to the idea that more help will be provided to the client, if needed. How the therapist proceeds will depend on whether they have both had the chance to preparc for the session. If they have, the therapist proceeds by asking the client about what has transpired since then. For example:

Therapist: Thank you for completing the pre-session preparation form and for sharing it with me. Would you mind if I refer to it as we proceed?

Client: No, that's fine

Therapist: Have you noticed what has changed for you since completing the form?

Client: I have been thinking about different ways of dealing with the issue.

Therapist: That's great, and I definitely want to hear your thoughts. But first, as this is the first time we have met to talk, I'd like to ask you, what is your understanding of the purpose of our conversation today?

Suppose the client has not done any preparation for the session. In that case, the therapist might begin by just asking the final question shown above ('What is your understanding of the purpose of our conversation today?').

If the client's response indicates an accurate understanding, the therapist proceeds with the session. If not, the therapist corrects any misunderstandings that the client may have, clarifies what they can do and what they can't do and asks the client if they want to proceed on that new basis.

- *The therapist asks the client what they would like help with*

  For example, the therapist may simply ask, 'What can I help you with today?' In response, the client usually begins to talk about the problem/issue/concern[11] for which they have come seeking help. If they have several problems, the therapist may ask the client to select the one with which they are currently preoccupied or the one that they are prepared to discuss today. Alternatively, the therapist might ask the client to identify any themes that may link their problems (e.g. fear of rejection). If such a theme is specified, the therapist will still work with the situation that currently preoccupies the client and will look for opportunities to apply learnings to the other theme-based situations as they both proceed. The therapist should aim to agree with the client concerning what will be the focus of the session.

- *The therapist asks the client what helping stance they could adopt that the client will find most helpful and give examples, if necessary*

---

[11] In this principle and the following one, I will the term 'problem'. However, the terms 'issue' and 'concern' are equally good synonyms and I suggest employing the term that the client uses in their response to the therapist's 'what can I help you with today' question.

In single-session therapy, no one 'helping stance' that the therapist can adopt will be universally therapeutic for all clients. Therefore, the therapist should ask the client to guide them on this point and be prepared to give examples. For example:

Therapist: Do you have a sense of how I can best help you today?

Client: I'm not sure.

Therapist: Well, I could help you focus on a problem and work with you to come up with a solution to the problem. I could help you to explore an issue so that you can get greater clarity on it. I could listen while you talk about an issue in your preferred way and help you get things off your chest. Or I could help you make a decision that you need to make or resolve a dilemma that you have. Which of these helping stances, as I call them, would suit you best?

It is understandable that the client may confuse the questions, 'what can I help you with today?' and 'how can I best help you today?'[12] Put simply, the difference is that the former question asks 'what', and the latter question asks 'how'. 'What' refers to problem content, while 'how' refers to helping stance.

---

[12] Even some therapists confuse the two!

- *The therapist helps the client to nominate a goal for the session rather than from therapy*

  Eliciting a session goal is what distinguishes SST from other modes of therapy delivery, where goal setting relates to the end of a course of therapy. A good question that a therapist can ask here is as follows: 'If, this evening, when you are at home, reflecting on our session today, and you concluded that you were glad you came to see me, what would you have realistically achieved from the session that would have led you to come to that conclusion?'

- *The therapist asks the client what they are prepared to sacrifice to achieve their goal*

  Depending on the goal that the client nominates, the therapist may ask them what they are ready to sacrifice to achieve their goal. For example, 'One-Session Treatment (OST) is a form of massed exposure therapy for the treatment of specific phobias. It combines exposure, participant modeling, cognitive challenges, and reinforcement in a single session, maximized to three hours' (Zlomke and Davis, 2008: 207). This involves the client being prepared to tolerate a fair measure of discomfort to benefit from the session. Those who are ready to do that sign up for the treatment programme and benefit from the extended session. Those who are not prepared to do that do not sign up for the programme!

- *The therapist helps the client to create a focus for the session and encourages them to keep to that focus*

  Having a focus for the session is a significant feature of effective SST practice. Such a focus needs to be jointly agreed upon by the therapist and client and reflects why the latter sought help. It is quite natural for a person to move away from a focus in therapy, as this happens in ordinary conversation. The best way to bring the client back to the agreed focus is to ask them at the outset for permission to interrupt them should they move away from the focus and do so as required.

- *The therapist strives to convey that they understand the client's nominated problem from the client's perspective*

  As I discussed in *Principle 5*, an important part of developing a good working relationship with the client is for the therapist to convey that they understand their nominated problem from the client's frame of reference. Doing so helps the client be more open to possible solutions to the problem than if they did not feel understood.

- *The therapist assesses the problem using whatever concepts they generally employ in problem-assessment*

  It is difficult for the therapist to help the person with their nominated problem without them both fully understanding it. In assessing the problem with the client, the therapist will use whatever framework they generally use to assess problems in therapy, with the difference that they will be as streamlined as possible and only focus on issues that are central to an accurate understanding of the problem. In *Principle 7*, I will show how I assess my clients' problems in SST.

- *The therapist bridges to the future whenever possible*

  It is often useful to assess a specific example of the client's nominated problem because such an example will most often yield the most accurate data. Since SST is forward-focused, I suggest that, if possible, the therapist asks the client to select a possible future example of the problem when assessing that problem. For example, if a client's nominated problem is fear of public speaking, the client should be asked, if possible, to select an instance in the near future when they are going to give a speech in public. Assessing a future example of a client's nominated problem will provide rich experiential data. It will also help the client implement whichever solution they select in the same situation in which the now assessed problem is deemed to occur. Thus:

> **Assess future example of the problem > select solution > apply in the same situation**

If the therapist assesses a past example of the client's nominated problem, they will then have to help the client to apply whatever solution the client thought would have been helpful in the *past* instance of the problem to the predicted *future* instance of the problem. Thus:

> **Assess past example of the problem > select solution > transfer to future situation**

In my view, the former is more efficient than the latter. However, it is important for the therapist to give the client a rationale for working with a future example of their nominated problem and give them a choice about which example to assess: a past example or a future example.

- *The therapist looks for ways of making an emotional impact without pushing for it*

  A productive session in SST is characterised by the client being emotionally and cognitively engaged in the discussion, using 'head' and 'heart' together, as it were. For this to happen, the therapist looks for ways of making the conversation have an emotional impact on the client. This needs to be natural and not forced. The therapist does this in several ways, including using the client's emotionally-related language and employing relevant images and metaphors. The therapist needs to avoid making the session an interesting intellectual chat or so emotional that the client becomes overwhelmed by affect and stops thinking.

- *The therapist uses questions constructively.*

  During SST, it is likely that the therapist will ask the client many questions. These questions are designed to help the client to focus on important elements of the problem and on the resources that the client can draw upon to address the problem effectively. Here it is important that the therapist gives the client time to answer questions and ensures, whenever possible, that the client answers the questions they are asked.

- *The therapist is clear in their communications*

  This includes, whenever practicable, the therapist explaining interventions, checking the client's understanding of substantive points and making clear how the client can access further help if needed.

- *The therapist encourages the client to be specific as possible but also to be mindful of opportunities for generalisation*

  In the time available to them in SST, the therapist and the client only have time to deal with a specific issue. However, it is still possible for the therapist to encourage the client to think about how they might generalise their learning to other issues with which they may be struggling.

- *The therapist helps the client to identify salient strengths and to apply them to their nominated problem, if relevant*

  Given the time-limited nature of SST, it is a productive use of time for the therapist to help the client identify strengths and inner resources that they can utilise to develop a solution to their nominated problem. If the client struggles with the concept of 'strengths', the therapist can provide them with some examples to prompt their thinking. If the client maintains that they have no strengths, the therapist can ask them to imagine being interviewed for a job they really want. With the proviso that they have to give an honest response, the therapist can ask the client what they would say at the interview if asked what strengths they have as a person. Would they respond, 'I have no strengths'? Hardly!

- *The therapist helps the client to identify environmental resources and to apply them to their nominated problem, if relevant*

  Such resources may include people on the client's 'team' who may provide support and other help, 'apps', self-help books, and relevant helping organisations.

- *The therapist identifies the client's history of trying to solve the problem*

  Before the therapist helps the client to develop a solution to their problem, it is important that they do not waste time discussing potential solutions that the client may have previously tried and failed to make work. Thus, it is useful for the therapist to identify the client's previous attempts to solve their problem, encouraging them to capitalise on successful attempts and discouraging them from using unsuccessful attempts.

- *The therapist undertakes solution-focused work with the client*

  In the SST context, I regard a solution as a measure implemented by the client that effectively addresses the nominated problem and helps the client work towards achieving their goal (see below).

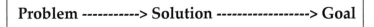

Problem ----------> **Solution** ------------------> **Goal**

  A solution may incorporate several relevant elements discussed in the session. These may include:

❑ The client's past attempts to deal with the problem that were helpful

❑ Relevant client strengths

❑ Environmental resources

❑ The opposite of problem-maintaining factors

❑ The client's ideas about what might contribute to a solution

❑ The therapist's ideas about what might contribute to a solution. Here the therapist offers the client their expertise without assuming the role of expert

In encouraging a client to select a solution with the client, it is vital that the therapist ensures that the client selects one that they will implement in their life. This will be a solution that they can easily integrate into their life. It may not necessarily be the solution that is most likely to be effective if selected. This critical point is worth reiterating. It is good practice for the therapist to encourage the client to choose an effective solution that they have a good chance of implementing because they can integrate it into their life.

• *The therapist encourages the client to rehearse the solution in the session*

If practicable, the therapist should help the client to rehearse the selected solution in the session. My shoe size is 8.5 wide fitting, and not many shoes are a comfortable fit for me. Consequently, whenever I buy a pair of shoes, I need to do so in a shop rather than online. Similarly, the client needs to discover if the selected solution is a 'good fit' for them. In the same way that a client will not implement a solution that they cannot easily integrate into their life, they will not implement a solution that does not 'fit' them. The therapist should work with the client until they have selected a solution that fits best. Ways of rehearsing the solution in the session include role play, imagery and chair-work (Kellogg, 2015). Rehearsing a solution helps the client realise whether or not a solution is a 'good fit'. It also helps them make modifications to one that does fit well (Dryden, 2019a).

- *The therapist helps the client to develop an action plan*

  After a solution has been selected, rehearsed, and, if necessary, modified, the therapist helps the client to develop a plan to implement the solution. This is not a specific 'homework assignment'. It is a broad action plan that shows a client what they need to do, when, where and how often. As with the solution itself, the client needs to develop a plan that they can integrate into their life.

- *The therapist encourages the client to identify and problem-solve potential obstacles to the implementation of the plan*

  Once the client has developed a suitable action plan, the therapist helps them to identify and address any barriers to the implementation of the plan. Doing so increases the chances that the client will deal effectively with the obstacles if they encounter them.

- *The therapist identifies and responds to the client's doubts, reservations and objections*

  Throughout the session, the therapist needs to be aware that the client may experience some doubts, reservations or objections (DROs) to salient aspects of the SST process. Such DROs tend to be expressed indirectly rather than directly (e.g., tone of voice or facial expression). Here is an example of how a therapist deals with a client DRO in SST.

  Therapist: I notice that when I asked you what you thought of that idea, although you said that you thought it was a good idea, the tone of your voice indicated that you might have a doubt.

  Client: Well, I guess so.

  Therapist: Can you share your reaction?

  Client: I wondered if I could see myself doing it

  Therapist: Thanks for sharing. Can you say a bit more?

  If the therapist does not allow the client to share and discuss any DROs they have, they will take them away from the session. These doubts, reservations, and objections may then impede the client from implementing the selected solution.

- *The therapist asks the client to summarise the session*

  One of the skills that a therapist learns during training is how to summarise portions of the session for the client. By contrast, in SST, the therapist encourages the client to summarise the work that the two of them have done, which most frequently occurs during the end phase of the session (see *Principle 4*). There are two reasons why a client summary is favoured in SST. First, it promotes the active stance that the therapist has encouraged the client to adopt throughout the session. Second, the client is more likely to be influenced by their own summary than by the therapist's summary going forward. The therapist may add to the client's summary if needed, but first, they need to validate how the client has synthesized the session.

- *The therapist encourages the client to take away 'one thing'*

  In *Principle 3,* I made the point that when a therapist brings a conventional clinical mindset to SST, they will tend to overload the client with the result that the client may become confused and lose focus about what they have learned from the session and thus what they can implement. By contrast, the SST practitioner operates on the idea that 'less is more' in SST and encourages the client to take away one thing that they have learned that is meaningful and that they can implement (Keller and Papasan, 2012). If the work has gone well, this will be the solution and an associated learning point.

- *Tie-up any loose ends*

  Before the session ends, it is important that the therapist helps the client to tie-up any loose ends. Remember that it is an important aspect of single-session thinking that there is an excellent ending to the session and that the client goes away with their morale restored, even if by a little. Tying-up loose ends involves (a) the therapist reminding the client of how they may access future help if needed (e.g. encouraging them to reflect and digest what they learned from the session, taking appropriate action, then waiting before deciding on further help), (b) inviting the client to ask any last-minute questions about the issue discussed or to tell the therapist something that they need to say before the close of the session, again about the issue discussed.

- *The therapist arranges to follow-up with the client*

  Before the therapist and client say their farewells, it is important for them to make an arrangement for the therapist to follow-up with the client. An agreed date should be made, and it should be made clear who is responsible for initiating the contact and how this is to be done.

There are those in the single-session therapy community who are purists and consider that SST should comprise the session and no other contact. For these people, follow-up is not a part of the SST process (see *Principle 4*). However, the consensual view in SST is that follow-up is an integral part of the process for the following reasons:

a. It allows the client to tell the therapist or agency representative[13] how they are getting on and whether they need further help. If so, this is organised.

b. It gives the therapist or agency representative feedback on what the SST process was like for the client, what was helpful for them, what was not so beneficial, what they got from the process and what they did not get from the process they hoped they would have gotten.

---

[13] Some people think that the therapist should be the one to follow-up the client while others hold that it should not be the therapist, but a representative of the agency in which the therapist works. The reason for the latter position is that the client is more likely to give honest feedback when speaking with someone that they have not met before. It is difficult for a client to give negative feedback to the therapist who they saw for SST.

c. It allows the agency to improve its SST service based on the client feedback about the agency's response to their application of help. For example, issues covered here might include what the client thought about the response time between application for help and that help being provided, how the agency responded to their initial contact, how the client preparing for the session was dealt with and how this could be improved.

*

In the following and final principle, I will discuss what individual therapists can bring to the SST process. In doing so, and for illustrative purposes, I will discuss what I bring to SST as an individual practitioner.

PRINCIPLE 7

Implementing Good Practice in SST:
II. Individual Contributions

In the previous principle, I outlined what I consider to be a consensual view of good practice in SST. These are ways of working that cut across different counselling and therapy approaches and can be viewed as common practical factors in single-session conversations.

However, it is also true to say that there is no one agreed way of practising SST. Thus, there is no agreed protocol for practice and no manual. There is, as a result, no 'adherence' scale for therapists to follow when research into SST is conducted.

What follows from this is that if a client were seen for a single planned session by three different therapists, the way the session would be conducted would be different in each case. Also, it would be feasible for the client to take away different things from each of the single sessions and be happy with each outcome.[14]

In what follows, I will draw on my SST practice to show how one therapist approaches single-session therapy. My practice comprises consensual-based practice (see *Principle 6)* and individual-based practice, as I will discuss. This equation (shown below) will be true for all SST practitioners.

> **SST Practice = Consensual-Based Practice (Common Factors) + Individual-Based Practice (Distinctive Factors)**

In the rest of the chapter, to illustrate the individual part of the above equation, I will describe the ideas, strategies and techniques that comprise the distinctive, individual-based way I practise SST. Remember that I will be outlining and discussing my unique way of thinking about and practising SST throughout this section. I recommend that you use this illustration to reflect on your practice of SST.

---

[14] This is consistent with pluralism and that is why, in my view, SST is an example of pluralistic practice (see Dryden, 2019a).

Utilising the Dynamics of Unhealthy and Healthy Negative Emotions

Most clients come to SST hoping for help with issues in which emotional problems often feature. When a client comes to me for SST, and they want help with an emotional problem, I bring to the conversation my knowledge of the eight major emotional problems for which people seek help: anxiety, depression, guilt, shame, hurt and the unhealthy forms of anger, jealousy and envy. Each of these emotions has accompanying behaviours and cognitions. I use this knowledge to inform my questions as I help my client and me understand their major emotional problem and how they act and think when they are experiencing the problem (Dryden, 2021a).

The theory of Rational Emotive Behaviour Therapy (REBT) states that for every unhealthy negative emotion (UNE), there is an alternative healthy negative emotion (HNE). Thus, the HNE alternatives to the UNEs listed above are: concern, sadness, remorse, disappointment, sorrow, and the healthy forms of anger, jealousy and envy (Dryden, 2021b). These healthy negative emotions also have a set of accompanying behaviours and cognitions, albeit more functional and constructive than those that accompany the UNEs (Dryden, 2021a). I use this information to help clients set realistic goals concerning their nominated problems, as I will elaborate on below.

Making an Accurate Assessment of the Client's Nominated Problem

I find that I devote much of the time in the session to making an accurate assessment of the client's problem. This involves identifying the major UNE and associated behaviours and cognitions, the adversity that mainly features in the client's problem and the attitude that accounts for the problem's existence (see below). Identifying the precise adversity is the most critical part of the problem assessment, for if I get this right, this will increase the chance that I will help the client find the best solution to their problem. In searching for the precise adversity, I use the information detailed in Table 7.1

Helping the Client Deal with the Main Adversity that Features in Their Nominated Problem

Helping the client to deal with the adversity that features in their nominated problem is one of the key ideas that I offer clients in SST when appropriate. For example, suppose my assessment of the client's nominated problem features a disturbed response to rejection (the adversity). In that case, my contribution to the client's goal-setting is to help them see the value of working towards feeling an HNE (with associated behaviours and cognitions) in response to this adversity rather than a UNE (with related actions and cognitions).

Table 7.1 Adversities with associated unhealthy and healthy negative emotions

Adversity	Negative emotions	
	Unhealthy	Healthy
– Threat	Anxiety	Concern
– Loss – Failure – Undeserved plight (experienced by self or others)	Depression	Sadness
– Breaking your moral code – Failing to abide by your moral code – Hurting someone	Guilt	Remorse
– Falling very short of your ideal in a social context – Others judging you negatively	Shame	Disappointment
– The other is less invested in your relationship than you – Someone betrays you or lets you down and you think you do not deserve such treatment	Hurt	Sorrow
– You or another transgresses a personal rule – Another disrespects you – Frustration	Unhealthy anger	Healthy anger
– Someone poses a threat to a valued relationship – You experience uncertainty related to this threat	Unhealthy jealousy	Healthy jealousy
– Others have what you value and lack	Unhealthy envy	Healthy envy

The critical point to realise here is that since the adversity (in this case, rejection) is negative when the client handles adversity well (which is their goal), they will still feel bad[15] about it. However, when they have this bad feeling, they will feel bad but not disturbed (HNE), and they will have accompanying balanced and non-ruminative ways of thinking and constructive ways of behaving. Contrast this to when they feel bad and disturbed (UNE). Here they will have accompanying highly distorted and ruminative forms of thinking and unconstructive ways of behaving (Dryden, 2021a).

Using Different Solutions with Different Clients

As I noted above, in my view, SST is an example of pluralistic practice. This idea underpins my view that different clients require and are likely to request different solutions.

Promoting Attitudinal Change Solutions

Having made the above point, I acknowledge that I favour attitudinal change solutions to client problems, all things being equal. This is based on the

---

[15] By feeling bad, I mean that the emotion has a negative experiential tone. Both UNEs and HNEs have this tone, but the former are disturbed in their effects while the latter tend to be constructive in their effects.

view that while what happens to a client contributes to their emotional problem, their attitude towards what happens to them contributes more and mainly accounts for the problem. If the client accepts this view, they will embrace the idea that they need to change their attitude to deal effectively with their problem. At this point, I will introduce an important principle of REBT that states that emotionally disturbed responses to adversities are based on rigid and extreme attitudes, and emotionally healthy responses to the same adversities are based on flexible and non-extreme attitudes. Suppose the client accepts this as the basis of a solution. In that case, I help them construct a suitable attitude and develop a plan concerning how they can implement this attitude after the session. This plan will likely be based on the idea that it is vital to act on attitudes to believe them rather than wait to believe these attitudes and then act on them.

Promoting Other Solutions

Not all clients will opt for an attitudinal solution to their problems. The pluralist in me fully accepts this, and therefore, I am ready to discuss a range of other solutions with the client in addition to those that they bring to the table (Dryden, 2019c). Such solutions include:

Inferential change solutions: Inferential change solutions are those that involve clients changing the inferences that they make about negative events. This occurs when a client considers the inference they have made and recognises that it did not fit the facts on balance. Consequently, they make a more realistic inference, leading them to deal more effectively with their problem.

Frame change solutions: Frame change solutions involve clients putting an entirely different, usually positive slant, on a way of viewing a situation. An example would be a client who sees that what they initially saw was an obstacle to their goals is, in fact, a great opportunity to be creative.

Behavioural change solutions: Behavioural change solutions are those that involve clients in changing their behaviour. Sometimes, such solutions may also lead to attitude change or inference change later.

Environmental change solutions: Environmental change solutions are so named because they describe when clients solve their problems by removing themselves from the negative situation that is the context for their emotional problem. An example of such a solution is where a client who has been suffering anxiety when bullied by their boss decides to leave their job.

Asking for Definitions

When a client uses a term that I am unclear about, I ask them to clarify what they mean, and I even ask for a definition of what they mean by the term, if necessary. I do this, particularly if I think that a term a client uses serves to maintain their problem. For example:

> *Client:* I want to ask her out for a date, but I just can't do it.
>
> *Windy:* I want to understand what you mean by the word 'can't' here. Do you mean that you don't have the ability to ask her out or that you do have the ability, but that it is hard for you to do?
>
> *Client*: I mean the latter.
>
> *Windy*: Does putting it like that change anything for you?
>
> *Client*: Yes, I can do it, but it's hard, as you say. That actually gives me some hope.

Pointing Out that 'Life is a Process'

I find it useful to use the idea that 'life is a process' with clients in SST. This leads me to ask a client, 'what happens next?' so that they can begin to see that a problematic event is the beginning of a process rather than the end of a process. Sometimes, I invite the client to regard the experience as 'Chapter 1' of a book and that they have the possibility of changing matters in the next or subsequent chapters.

Emphasizing the Power of the Second and Subsequent Response

A related concept to the 'life is a process' idea is that the client's first response is not the problem. It is how they respond to this first response. Thus, if a client responds with anxiety to an adversity, I want to convey to them, this is understandable. Still, it is how they respond to anxiety that determines whether they have a problem or not. With some clients, I distinguish between a reaction – which is immediate and unconsidered – and a response – which happens after a period of consideration. Once I have made this distinction with such clients, I say that their problem is not in how they react but in how they respond to how they react.

The Problem is Not in the Urge but in How You Respond to the Urge

Often, clients think that their problem is that they experience an urge to do something self-defeating since they believe that they have to act on it if they have an urge.

Consequently, they consider that they have to get rid of the urge. Urge elimination then becomes part of the problem rather than part of the solution. Instead, I make the point that an urge only gets converted into action by the person's decision to act on the urge. Instead, the client can stand back from the urge and choose a considered course of action. In doing so, they have to tolerate the ensuing discomfort that often accompanies not acting on an urge.

Helping the Client to Focus on What They Can Control, Rather Than on What They Can't Control

As I made clear in *Principles 3 and 5,* the therapist needs to be transparent with the client about what they, the therapist, can do and can't do in SST. Similarly, the therapist needs to help the client see what they, the client, can control and what they can't control in their life. Using this point, I will help the client to select and focus on an issue in the session where they can exert some control.

You Can't Change Another Person, But You Can Influence Them

The 'focus on what you can control' principle is particularly relevant to a situation in which a client's problem involves another person. In such a case, I help the client see that while they cannot change another person, they can attempt to influence that person. Their influence attempts are within their control. While taking this tack, I help the client acknowledge that the other person does not have to listen to them or be influenced by them.

Helping the Client View Their Options and the Consequences of These Options Before They Make a Choice

When a client nominates a problem that involves them ultimately making a choice, I find it productive at the outset to help them look at all their options in a given situation and ask them to consider the consequences, both in the short- and long-term of each option. Once they have made a choice, then one of two things will occur. First, the client will have arrived at the solution that they were looking for because they feel able to implement their choice in their life. Second, although the client has selected the best option, they experience an obstacle to implementing it. When this happens, we agree to focus on the obstacle, and I help the client deal effectively with the obstacle in the session so that they are prepared to deal with it in their life should they encounter it.

Encouraging the Client to Accept the Presence of a Painful Emotion or Thought Rather than Attempt to Eliminate It

Sometimes, the client's problem is exacerbated by their wish to eliminate the unhealthy negative emotion or negative thinking they experience in the problem state. We know that attempts to eradicate thinking have the effect of maintaining it (Wegner. 1994), and we also know, for example, that trying to eliminate anxiety leads to it increasing as the person becomes anxious about their anxiety (Ellis, 1979, 1980). Instead, I encourage the client to accept (but not like) such thoughts and feelings and to move forward based on such acceptance.

Encouraging the Client to Act in the Absence of Preferred Conditions

Often clients prevent themselves from solving their emotional problems by thinking that they need certain preferred conditions to be present before they take constructive action. Rather than waiting for such favourable conditions to exist before acting, I encourage such people to act in the absence of these conditions. Additionally, I encourage them to act in the presence of unfavourable conditions. I find this a particularly useful approach in helping people in SST to address procrastination issues.

Helping Clients to Use Goals and Values to Guide Action

The final point I want to make is that I encourage clients in SST to use their long-term goals and values to guide their behaviour. This is particularly helpful when a client is caught up with short-term considerations at the expense of longer-term considerations. Thus, when a person is experiencing discomfort and is tempted to avoid doing something that is in their long-term best interests, suggesting that they use their relevant long-term goals and/or their values to guide them in their decision-making can be particularly therapeutic.

*

We have reached the end of this book, but before closing, I will provide some further reading suggestions for those wishing to learn more about single-session therapy. I hope you have found this book of value. If you have any feedback, please email me at windy@windydryden.com

APPENDIX 1

An SST Leaflet that I Send Out to Potential Clients

What is Single-Session Therapy (SST)?

Information for Prospective Clients

Windy Dryden PhD

- Single-Session Therapy is an intentional endeavour where you and I set out with the purpose of helping you in one session, on the understanding that more help is available

- In SST, therapy takes place one contact at a time, and one contact may be all the time that you need. At the end of the session, I will invite you to reflect on and digest what you learned in the session, act on what you learned and see what happens before deciding whether to seek another session. In SST, a block of sessions is not offered routinely to you but can be done so, if you and I decide that this is indicated

- SST is based on the principle of offering help at the point of need rather than at the point of availability. It has the effect of you being seen quickly, when you need help

- SST is based on three foundations:
  - The most frequent number of sessions clients have internationally is '1', followed by '2', '3', and so on
  - 70-80% of those who have one session are satisfied with that session given their current circumstances
  - Therapists are poor at predicting who will attend for only one session and who will attend for more

- My goals in SST are:
  - To help you get 'unstuck'
  - To help you take a few steps forward which may encourage you to travel the rest of the journey without my professional assistance
  - To help you address a specific issue

- If you want to prepare for the session, I will help you to do this either by sending you a questionnaire for you to complete or by having a brief telephone conversation with you

- The focus of a session in SST is on us negotiating a goal for the session after which I will help you to find and rehearse a solution that facilitates the achievement of this goal. Then, I will help you to devise an action plan which you can implement after the session.

- In SST, I will help you to:
  - Discover what you have done in the past to deal with your problem. I will then encourage you to use what has been helpful and set aside what has not been helpful
  - Identify and use your internal strengths and external resources in implementing the agreed solution

- I encourage follow-up to discover how you are getting on and to improve service delivery and at the end of the session we will make an appointment for a follow-up

APPENDIX 2

Narration Accompanying My Whiteboard Animation on Single-Session Therapy

(https://www.youtube.com/watch?v=wIcuOVOABRw)[16]

- Amy has an emotional problem she wants help with. Imagine these two scenarios.

- Scenario 1: Amy consults her GP who refers her to a local clinic. She is assessed, offered an appointment and her therapy begins about 12 weeks after she first sought help. This is known as 'Help provided at the point of availability'

- Scenario 2: Amy goes to a walk-in clinic, completes a brief form and sees a therapist 30 minutes later. This is known as 'Help provided at the point of need'

- Help provided at the point of need is delivered by a way of working with clients known as Single-Session Therapy which can be accessed by walk-in or by appointment

- Single-Session Therapy occurs when the therapist and client meet with the agreed intention of addressing the client's problem in one session so that the client can move forward on their own. However, it is also agreed that more sessions are available to the client if needed

- Single-Session Therapy is a way of delivering therapy services which is based on three main points:

    1. Across the world, the most frequent number of sessions clients have is 1, followed by 2, followed by 3 etc.

---

[16] Accessed on 12 February 2021.

2. 70-80% of clients who attend for one session are satisfied with the session given their current circumstances
3. Therapists are poor at predicting who will attend for one session and who will attend for more

- Single-Session Therapy is best integrated with other services within a therapy agency. One way of doing this is to offer everyone who needs help an immediately available single session. Those who need additional help, or a different service can have it, but, where appropriate, everybody is encouraged to engage in a five-stage process before seeking another session:

  - First, they reflect on what they learned from the session
  - Second, they digest this learning
  - Third, they act on the learning
  - Fourth, they let time pass and
  - Finally, they decide if they need another session

- In Single-Session Therapy, the therapist does the following:

  - First, they help the client to identify past attempts to solve the problem, encouraging them to build on what was helpful and cast aside what was not helpful
  - Second, they encourage the client to identify and use their inner strengths and resiliency factors while addressing their problem
  - Third, they encourage the client to identify and use external resources, such as supportive people in their environment while addressing the problem

- During the session itself, the therapist works with the client to identify the best available solution to the problem. The client is encouraged to rehearse the solution in the session before drawing up an action plan to implement the solution

- At the end of the session, the therapist reminds the client that more help is available if needed

APPENDIX 3

An Example of a Pre-Session Preparation Questionnaire

Pre-session Questionnaire

I invite you to fill in this questionnaire before your single session with me. It is a very important part of the process so please engage with the questions as much as you can. I have found that it helps people to prepare for their session with me so that they can get the most from it. It also helps me to help you as effectively as I can. Please return it by email attachment before our session.

1. What is the single most important issue you would like help with now?

2. How is this affecting your life presently?

3. What would you like to achieve by the end of the <u>session</u> that would give you the sense that you had begun to make progress?

4. What have you done in the past that has helped even in a small way with the issue? Include your own attempts to help yourself and any therapy you have received on the issue.

5. What have you tried that has not helped with the issue? Again, please include your own attempts to help yourself and any therapy you have received on the issue.

6. Who in your life can support you as you tackle the issue now?

---

7. What strengths do you have as a person that may help you to address the issue?

---

8. Is there anything you think that it is vital for me to know in order to be able to help you with the issue?

Thank you.

Windy Dryden, PhD

Further Reading

I recommend starting with the book that generated much interest in single-session therapy when it first came out and continues to do so. It puts SST in a historical context:

- Talmon, M. (1990). *Single Session Therapy: Maximising the Effect of the First (and Often Only) Therapeutic Encounter*. San Francisco: Jossey-Bass.

For those seeking a comprehensive guide to the theory and practice of single-session therapy, I suggest:

- Dryden, W. (2019). *Single-Session Therapy: 100 Key Points and Techniques*. Abingdon, Oxon: Routledge.

For those looking for a client SST workbook that can be used in conjunction with therapy or by clients on their own, I suggest:

- Dryden, W. (2021). *Help Yourself with Single-Session Therapy*. Abingdon, Oxon: Routledge.

The following three edited texts provide state-of-the-art information on SST theory, practice and research:

- Hoyt, M. F. and Talmon, M. F. (eds) (2014). *Capturing the Moment: Single Session Therapy and Walk-In Services*. Bethel, CT: Crown House Publishing.
- Hoyt, M. F., Bobele, M., Slive, A., Young, J., and Talmon, M. (eds) (2018). *Single-Session Therapy by Walk-In or Appointment: Administrative, Clinical, and Supervisory Aspects of One-at-a Time Services*. New York: Routledge.
- Hoyt, M. F., Young, J., and Rycroft, P. (eds) (2021). *Single Session Thinking and Practice in Global, Cultural and Familial Contexts: Expanding Applications*. New York: Routledge.

References

Appelbaum, S. A. (1975). Parkinson's Law in psychotherapy. *International Journal of Psychoanalytic Psychotherapy, 4,* 426–36.

Bloom, B. L. (1981). Focused single-session therapy: Initial development and evaluation. In S. Budman (ed.), *Forms of Brief Therapy* (pp. 167–216). New York: Guilford Press.

Bordin, E. S. (1979). The generalizability of the psychoanalytic concept of the working alliance. *Psychotherapy: Theory, Research and Practice, 16,* 252–60.

Brown, G.. S. and Jones, E. R. (2005). Implementation of a feedback system in a managed care environment: What are patients teaching us? *Journal of Clinical Psychology, 61,* 187–98.

Dryden, W. (2011). *Counselling in a Nutshell. 2nd edition.* London: Sage.

Dryden, W. (2017). *Single-Session Integrated CBT (SSI-CBT): Distinctive Features.* Abingdon, Oxon: Routledge.

Dryden, W. (2018). *Very Brief Therapeutic Conversations.* Abingdon, Oxon: Routledge.

Dryden, W. (2019a). *Single-Session Coaching and One-At-A-Time Coaching: Distinctive Features.* Abingdon, Oxon: Routledge.

Dryden, W. (2019b). *Single-Session Therapy: 100 Key Points and Techniques.* Abingdon, Oxon: Routledge.

Dryden, W. (2021a). *Understanding Emotional Problems and Their Healthy Alternatives. 2nd edition.* Abingdon, Oxon: Routledge.

Dryden, W. (2021b). *Rational Emotive Behaviour Therapy: Distinctive Features. 3rd edition.* Abingdon, Oxon: Routledge.

Dryden, W. (2021c). *Seven Principles of Rational Emotive Behaviour Therapy.* London: Rationality Publications.

Ellis, A. (1979). Discomfort anxiety: A new cognitive behavioral construct. Part I . *Rational Living, 14*(2), 3–8.

Ellis, A. (1980). Discomfort anxiety: A new cognitive behavioral construct. Part 2. *Rational Living, 15*(1), 25–30.

Findlay, R. (2007). A mandate for honesty, Jeff Young's No Bullshit Therapy: An interview. *Australian and New Zealand Journal of Family Therapy, 28*(3), 165–70.

Frank, J. D. (1961). *Persuasion and Healing: A Comprehensive Study of Psychotherapy*. Baltimore, MD: The Johns Hopkins Press.

Garvin, C. D. and Seabury, B. A. (1997). *Interpersonal Practice in Social Work: Promoting Competence and Social Justice. 2nd Edition*. Boston, MA: Allyn & Bacon.

Hoyt, M. F. (2000). *Some Stories are Better than Others: Doing What Works in Brief Therapy and Managed Care*. Philadelphia: Brunner/Mazel.

Hoyt, M. F. (2018). Single-session therapy: Stories, structures, themes, cautions, and prospects. In M. F. Hoyt, M. Bobele, A. Slive, J. Young, and M. Talmon (eds), *Single-Session Therapy by Walk-In or Appointment: Administrative, Clinical, and Supervisory Aspects of One-at-a-Time Services* (pp. 155–74). New York: Routledge.

Hoyt, M. F. and Rosenbaum, R. (2018). Some ways to end an SST. In M. F. Hoyt, M. Bobele, A. Slive, J. Young, and M. Talmon (eds), *Single-Session Therapy by Walk-In or Appointment: Administrative, Clinical, and Supervisory Aspects of One-at-a Time Services* (pp. 318–23). New York: Routledge.

Hoyt, M. F. and Talmon, M. F. (2014a). What the literature says: An annotated bibliography. In M. F. Hoyt and M. Talmon (eds), *Capturing the Moment: Single Session Therapy and Walk-In Services* (pp. 487–516). Bethel, CT: Crown House Publishing.

Hoyt, M. F. and Talmon, M. F. (eds) (2014b). *Capturing the Moment: Single Session Therapy and Walk-In Services*. Bethel, CT: Crown House Publishing.

Hoyt, M.F., Young, J., and Rycroft, P. (2020). Single session thinking 2020. *Australian & New Zealand Journal of Family Therapy, 41*(3), 218–30.

Keller, G. and Papasan, J. (2012). *The One Thing: The Surprisingly Simple Truth Behind Extraordinary Results*. Austin, TX: Bard Press.

Kellogg, S. (2015) *Transformational Chairwork: Using Psychotherapeutic Dialogues in Clinical Practice*. Lanham, MD: Rowman & Littlefield.

Norcross, J. C. and Cooper, M. (2021). *Personalizing Psychotherapy: Assessing and Accommodating Patient Preferences*. Washington, DC: American Psychological Association.

Rogers, C. R. (1957). The necessary and sufficient conditions of therapeutic personality change. *Journal of Consulting Psychology, 21*, 95–103.

Simon, G. E., Imel, Z. E., Ludman, E. J., and Steinfeld, B. J. (2012). Is dropout after a first psychotherapy visit always a bad outcome? *Psychiatric Services, 63*(7), 705–7.

Slive, A. and Bobele, M. (eds) (2011). *When One Hour Is All You Have: Effective Therapy for Walk-in Clients.* Phoenix, AZ: Zeig, Tucker & Theisen.

Slive, A., McElheran, N., and Lawson, A. (2008). How brief does it get? Walk-in single session therapy. *Journal of Systemic Therapies, 27*, 5–22.

Talmon, M. (1990). *Single Session Therapy: Maximising the Effect of the First (and Often Only) Therapeutic Encounter.* San Francisco: Jossey-Bass.

Wegner, D. M. (1994). *White Bears and Other Unwanted Thoughts: Suppression, Obsession and the Psychology of Mental Control.* New York: Guilford Press.

Young, J. (2018). SST: The misunderstood gift that keeps on giving. In M. F. Hoyt, M. Bobele, A. Slive, J. Young, J., and M. Talmon, (eds), *Single-Session Therapy by Walk-In or Appointment: Administrative, Clinical, and Supervisory Aspects of One-at-a Time Services* (pp. 40–58). New York: Routledge.

Young, K. and Bhanot-Malhotra, S. (2014). *Getting Services Right: An Ontario Multi-Agency Evaluation Study.* www.excellenceforchildandyouth.com

Young, K. and Jebreen, J. (2019). Recognising single-session therapy as psychotherapy. *Journal of Systemic Therapies, 38*(4), 31–44.

Zlomke, K. and Davis, T. E. (2008). One-session treatment of specific phobias: a detailed description and review of treatment efficacy. *Behaviour Therapy, 39,* 207–23.

Index

Page numbers in bold refer to main principles.

Index

CPSIA information can be obtained
at www.ICGtesting.com
Printed in the USA
LVHW081435300321
682964LV00033B/504

9 781910 301920